COLOROBICS

Mindfulness coloring exercises for kids

Dr Stan Rodski

Peak Performance Neuroscientist

Hardie Grant

BOOKS

introduction

Everyone feels different emotions at different times. There will be days where you may feel happy or excited. Other days you may feel a little flat or worried. All this is quite normal, unless a feeling stays for too long or starts to affect others around you.

Colorobics is based on the idea that colors can affect how we feel and how we behave. The pictures in this book will help you get creative and use color to change the way you feel – the combination of colors you use can either relax or energize your brain. As you color in the pictures, you'll create patterns and make your brain feel good.

Let's get started with Colorobics!

Look at the opposite page. What colors do you like? Pick a color or two, then turn the page to find out what your color choice tells you about how you feel today.

Colorobics© is a technique developed by Dr Stan Rodski based on the idea that colors can affect our emotions and improve our wellbeing and mental health.

COLOROBICS

Mindfulness coloring exercises for kids

pick a color

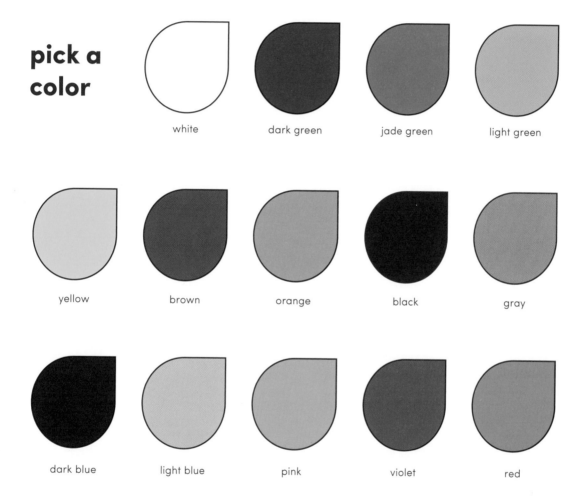

white

dark green

jade green

light green

yellow

brown

orange

black

gray

dark blue

light blue

pink

violet

red

how do I feel?

Look for the color you chose below and see how you feel today.

bored
white

tense
black

a little relaxed
dark green

nervous
gray

average
jade green

happy
dark blue

unsettled
light green

calm
light blue

imaginative
yellow

worried
pink

restless
brown

focused
violet

daring
orange

excited
red

the colorobic technique

Now that you know how you feel, you can use Colorobics to either change the way you feel or to help you feel that way for longer.

Here are three feelings you might like to experience, and the colors that can help you feel that way.

If you want to feel RELAXED, use these colors:

light blue   dark blue   jade green   dark green

If you want to feel EXCITED, use these colors:

red   orange   yellow

If you want to feel HAPPY, use these colors:

dark blue   yellow   dark green   violet

Once you decide how you want to feel, choose a picture and start coloring, using the colors connected to that feeling.

Use the colors to create patterns if you can. Remember, you don't have to finish the whole picture. There is no competition here – it's not a race, and there's no right or wrong. Just be creative and enjoy yourself.

Practice the Colorobics technique as often as you want to and for as long as you like. Your mood may change, along with your emotions and how you go about your day.

Enjoy your Colorobics workout – your brain will thank you.

Dr Stan Rodski
Neuroscientist

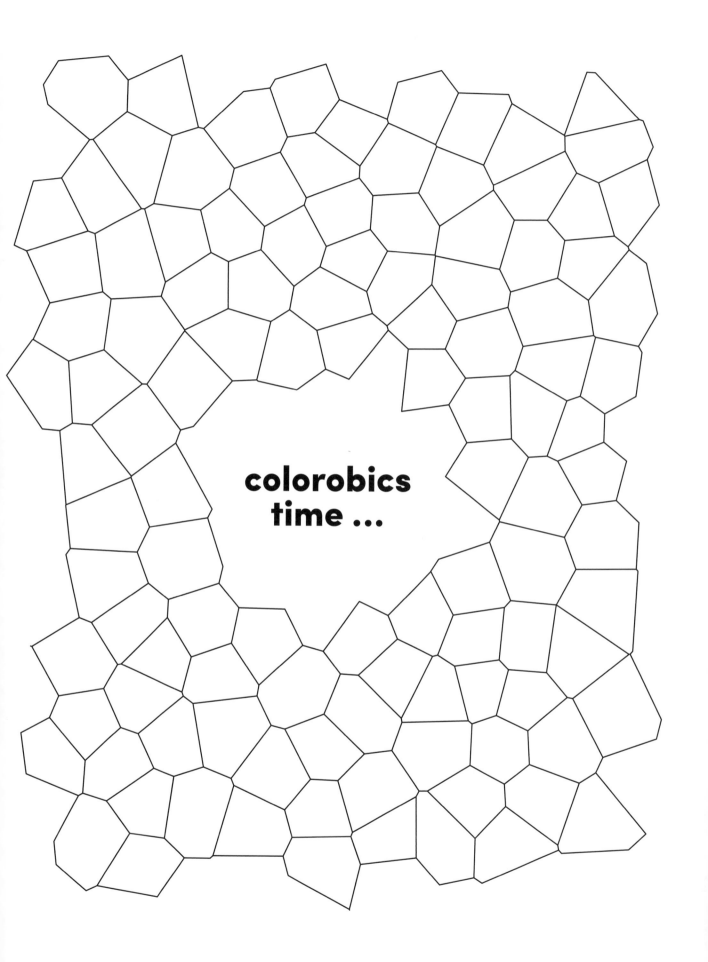

colorobics
time ...

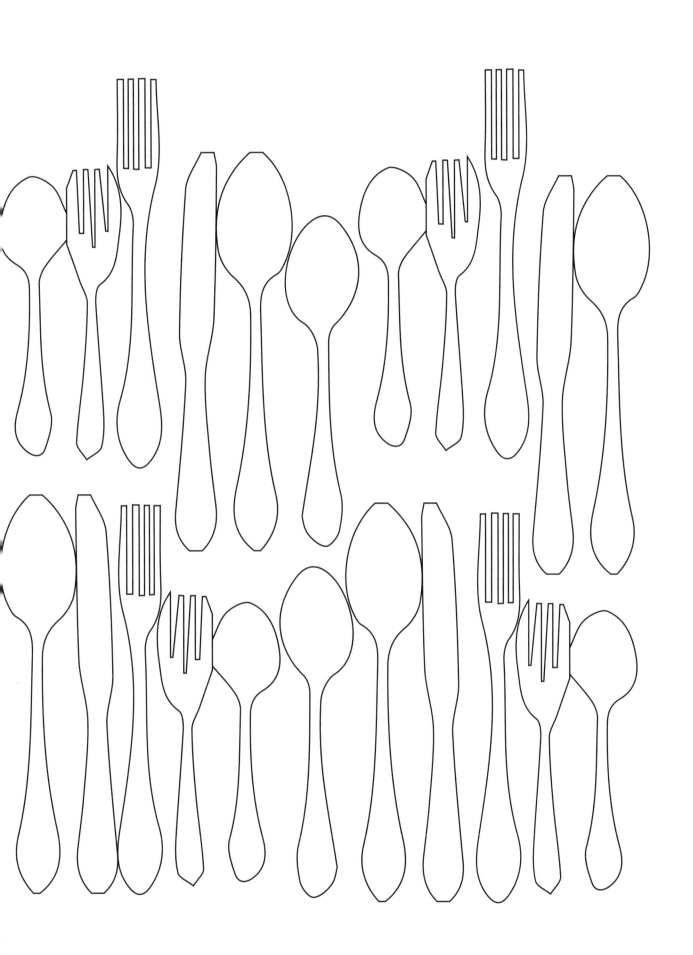

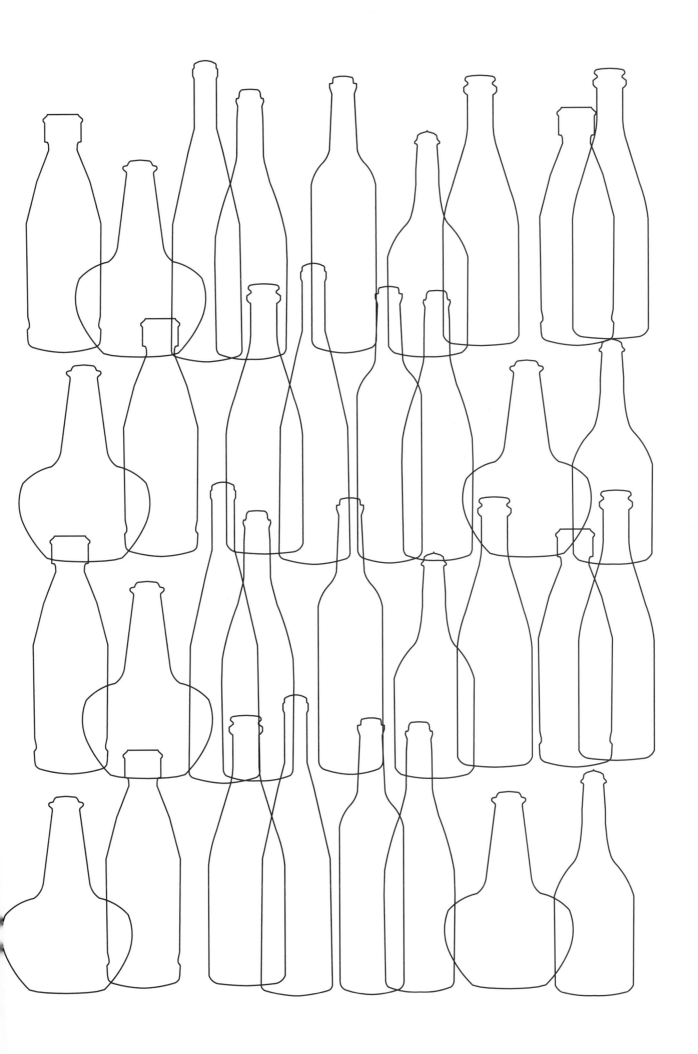

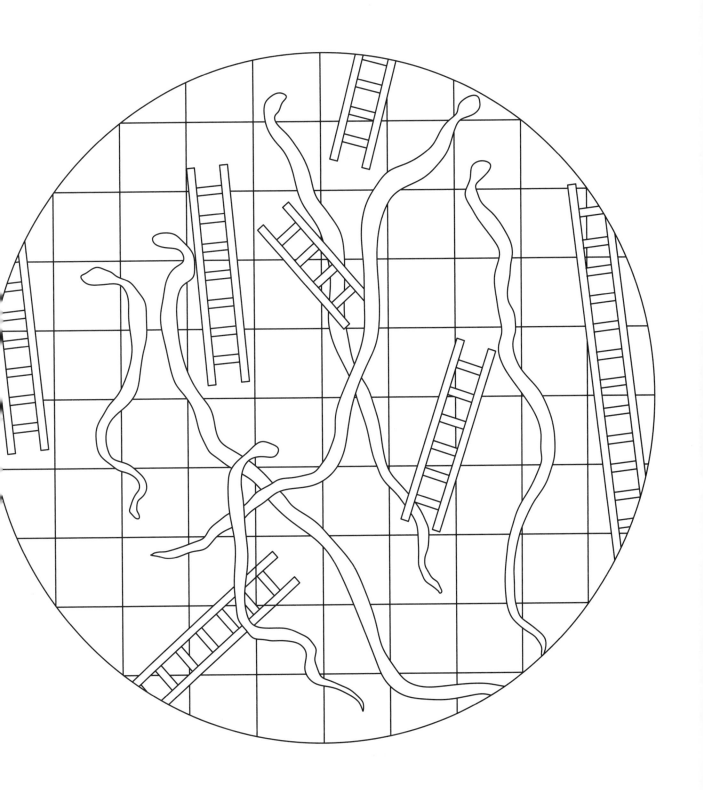

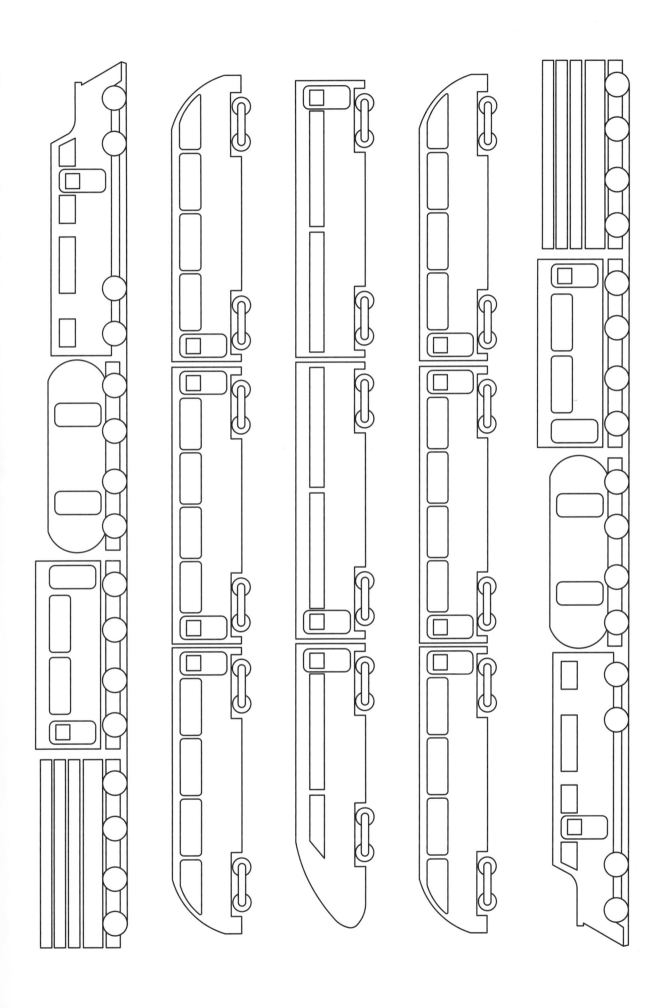

Dr Stan Rodski has worked as a psychologist for more than 30 years and has been involved in neuroscience research around stress and anxiety. Based in Melbourne, Australia, he has applied his research in various areas of improving wellbeing, such as sleep, fatigue and stress, as well as energy management and revitalization. Dr Rodski has worked with individuals, children, sporting teams and many top 500 companies in Australia and internationally.

Published in 2022 by Hardie Grant Books, an imprint of Hardie Grant Publishing

Hardie Grant Books (Melbourne)
Wurundjeri Country
Building 1, 658 Church Street
Richmond, Victoria 3121

Hardie Grant Books (London)
5th & 6th Floors
52–54 Southwark Street
London SE1 1UN

hardiegrantbooks.com

 A catalogue record for this book is available from the National Library of Australia

Colorobics
ISBN 978 1 74379 816 4

10 9 8 7 6 5 4 3 2 1

Publisher: Pam Brewster
Project Editor: Joanna Wong
Editor: Vanessa Lanaway
Design Manager: Kristin Thomas
Cover Designer: Reg Abos
Typesetter: Patrick Cannon
Production Manager: Todd Rechner
Production Coordinator: Jessica Harvie

Color reproduction by Splitting Image Colour Studio
Printed in China by Leo Paper Products LTD.

 The paper this book is printed on is from FSC®-certified forests and other sources. FSC® promotes environmentally responsible, socially beneficial and economically viable management of the world's forests.

Hardie Grant acknowledges the Traditional Owners of the country on which we work, the Wurundjeri people of the Kulin nation and the Gadigal people of the Eora nation, and recognizes their continuing connection to the land, waters and culture. We pay our respects to their Elders past, present and emerging.